Cat Care

The Essential Guide

ROB DUFFY SERIES EDITOR

Published in Great Britain in 2019 by
need2know
Remus House
Coltsfoot Drive
Peterborough
PE2 9BF
Telephone 01733 898103
www.need2knowbooks.co.uk

Contents

Introduction

So, you have recently brought a cat into your home as a new family member or are considering doing so. In this book, we take a close look at what it means to be responsible for one of these wonderful animals. People who have cats as pets usually find their lives are completely transformed, and can't imagine life without at least one cat in it. Single people, families, young and old, all find that having a cat around brings huge rewards, not all of which they can explain.

If you're a cat lover, you'll know there's nothing in the world like it. For those who don't get it, cats seem like lazy, ungrateful animals who wander in and out of your house when they're hungry. Worse, when they get bored, they rip your furniture to bits. These kind of observations usually come from cat owners, or people who prefer their pets docile. To a cat lover, the fact that they do what they want means they're healthy, curious and really alive.

Cats are clean, clever and remarkably self-sufficient. They are also extremely sensitive to their environment, including you, their owner. They will know when something is wrong and pick up on it, possibly before they enter the home. Cats have been shown to detect human illnesses way before people notice any symptoms themselves. Looking after a cat really means helping it to help itself. This two way relationship is extremely rewarding, and also very low-maintenance most of the time.

Science has also confirmed that owners of cats usually are less stressed out, often because of the affection they receive from their cat. There seems to be a myth out there that dogs are more affectionate than cats. That's just not true. Cats replicate human partner behavior in many ways. In fact, they're better at it, because they always make the first move, and always repay favors. Cats really do have long memories, and return all the affection they receive. If you're looking for a good companion, you have made an excellent decision in choosing a cat.

Things to Know About Owning A Cat

While owning a new cat can be exciting it can also be perplexing at times, and there are many considerations for owning a cat, whatever the breed. Here are a few top tips to get you started and some further insight into the implications of owning a cat.

Microchip

There are numerous decisions to be made with your pet. One such decision is whether to microchip your cat. Most cat charities urge cat owners to microchip their cat to help the cat be reunited with their owner if the cat becomes lost. All around the world, there are issues with stray cats. This is not just due to cats being dumped. It is partly because there is no way to reunite lost cats with their owners without proper identification. If you microchip your cat and they get out, and someone picks them up, it is likely either the vet, animal warden or charity who picks your cat up will be able to reunite you with your beloved pet. One quick scan for a microchip and your information pops up.

Most cat charities urge cat owners to microchip their cat to help the cat be reunited with their owner if the cat becomes lost.

Vaccinations

As a new cat owner, you will want to keep in mind that your cat will need vaccinations and regular check-ups with the vet. This is an added, but necessary, expense on top of daily food and water. Vaccinations are important, which we will discuss further in the first chapter. Make sure your cat's vaccinations are kept up as recommended as it could literally save their life.

Pet Insurance

Pet insurance is another option to consider. Most pet-insurers do not cover pre-existing health conditions or vaccinations. There are a few that do. It is important to look up several insurers online and check to see what they cover for the amount you will pay each month. However, if your cat needs an unexpected operation, pet insurance can come in handy as many people cannot afford to pay such a large sum at once. You would need to think carefully about whether you could afford an unforeseen large vet bill if it came up.

Cats are prone to cancer, diabetes, Feline Immunodeficiency Virus (FIV), Feline Leukemia Virus (FLV), heartworm, rabies, ringworm and Urinary Tract Infections (UTRs). These things happen, and it is good to be prepared.

Weight

Obesity in cats is on the rise these days. Some cat breeds are at high risk for obesity. Their natural instincts to roam and explore can be stifled by over-protectiveness. This reduces the amount of vital exercise these inquisitive creatures need. If you over feed your cat and do not let them out enough, you will have issues with obesity. Obesity can make health problems, such as lung, joint and heart issues worse for your cat. It is important to figure out what you will be feeding your cat. Also, if your cat starts to gain too much weight as an adult, you need to know what to do about it. Avoiding feeding your cat kitchen and table scraps is one good way. Also, having a regular feeding schedule can be effective. Many times, people give their cats treats to make their cat happy. Sometimes, instead of a treat, a good petting or stroking can make your cat feel like they have received a treat and it is a good bonding experience between you both.

Exercise

Cats thrive on exercise. This is sometimes easy to forget, as your cat may seem happiest when it is doing nothing. In fact, its senses are alert at all times, and you will usually find that your cat grooms itself, ready for its next adventure. You will also notice that your cat can turn from a dozing fluff ball into a blur of speed at a moment's notice. This is because cats are wired to react quickly. They must be encouraged to explore their local environment, and not kept captive in the home. Have a cat flap fitted so your pet can escape and come back as it sees fit. Cats will let you overindulge them, so don't.

Food

Sometimes it can seem complicated knowing what is okay and what is not to feed your cat. There are many foods that can make your cat ill or even kill them. Chocolate is not the only dangerous food, although it is the most talked about. It can be challenging to keep your cat from eating human food, especially if there are other members of your household around such as children. Some foods that may seem harmless, like caffeine, raisins, and grapes can get your cat very sick. It is important to let children know not to feed the cat anything without asking you first.

Grooming

Cat owners can be forgiven for being confused when it comes to grooming their pet. Cats are notorious for keeping themselves clean, and most spend a lot of time doing so. They have rasping tongues which can dislodge just about anything from their fur, paws, nails or anywhere else on their bodies. By licking their paws, they can also reach behind their ears and clean their faces, which is better than some children! That doesn't mean that you as a cat owner have to leave well alone when it comes to your pet's grooming. Longer haired breeds especially might welcome some help. Also, less agile or unfit cats might not be able to take care of themselves as they normally would. If you approach your cat correctly, especially early in your relationship, you may find it easier than you expect to initiate a bond which enables you to help your cat with its grooming regime. This can help both of you, in a number of ways.

Even if you have a short-haired cat, a regular brush once a week is a positive step to take. This helps get rid of anything your cat has missed, and gets your pet used to your attention. It will also feel cleaner afterwards, which it always enjoys. Cats with longer hair can benefit from a daily brushing, as dead hairs quickly build up. Remember, long haired breeds of cat have been specially bred this way; their tongues are not designed to cope with this extra amount of hair. Matting is a common problem caused by insufficient grooming. Hair sticks and knots together, especially in certain areas of your cat's body. Once matting starts, it can quite quickly become uncomfortable for your pet, and matted hair can harbor diseases, bacteria and small insects, which your cat won't be able to dislodge.

If you have a short-haired cat, use a fine-toothed comb, once a week. Comb in the direction of your cat's fur, going with the nap. This will gently separate the hairs without irritating or hurting the skin underneath. For longer haired cats, you'll need a steel comb, as plastic will bend too easily. Use it once a day, and look out for matting. If you come across matting or knots, try to ease them out gently, using a damp cloth if necessary. For particularly difficult areas, take your cat to the vet for help. You can also use grooming time to check your cat's claws, paws and teeth. Older or inactive cats can experience problems caused by overgrowing claws quite quickly. These can become ingrown, leading to pain and possible infection. Similarly, while your cat is in your control, lift its gums and have a look for any obvious problems with its teeth.

Health

Your cat's health can become a confusing matter. There are vaccinations that are needed at certain times in a cat's life, not just when they are kittens. You also need to know when your cat will need worming. Flea and tick control for your cat are very important as fleas and ticks can make your cat ill. Some ticks can even get humans ill. It is also good to know some basic cat first aid to use before you bring your cat to the vet for a hurt or cut paw.

A New Family Member

This book has a lot of information that you will find helpful and useful when owning a cat. This will assist you in taking the best care of your cat so that you can have a fulfilling life together. These helpful tips will help you feel more confident with your beloved new family member. Having a feline friend in your family, especially an inquisitive, active and fun cat, can help you build many fond and happy memories.

There are vaccinations that are needed at certain times in a cat's life, not just when they are kittens.

The Kitten

Getting a kitten sounds like a cute and fun idea. Domestic kittens are adorable and can be lots of fun. It is good to keep in mind the practical aspects of having one. Kittens need a lot of observation, time, awareness and care. Socializing kittens is very important also to keep them from being anxious or badly behaved when they meet other cats. Very young cats, like most adult cats, have a lot of energy. They are intelligent, curious animals finding out about the world around them.

Time to kitten-proof your home

Kittens are known to chew and scratch almost everything they see. You will need to kitten-proof your home which means getting pretty much any item they can damage out of your kitten's way.

- Make sure to move away any rugs you might have on the floor. Kittens will chew on them and drag them around.

- Any small objects such as keys, coins, marbles, jewelry, needles, pens, screws, pins, buttons or tiny bouncy balls need to be kept away from kittens as they can swallow them. This can be dangerous as they can choke or need a visit to the vet to remove the items if they get stuck in their digestive tract.

- As with small children, you need to literally lock away medications and cleaning products. Keep them up where your kitten cannot reach them as they can chew through containers.

- Until your kitten is trained not to jump up and take food, it is important to not leave food on counter tops or tables as your kitten will steal it.

- Any heavy objects that can be knocked over need to be taken away from the area your kitten is in. A heavy object falling can cause serious injury to your kitten.

- Kittens tend to chew everything, and that includes electrical cables. Keep them away by putting them in a cable tidy, or you can use sturdy masking tape to tape cables to the wall.

- Please make it clear to your children that they cannot leave chocolate anywhere that a kitten can get to it. Chocolate has been known to kill both adult cats and kittens.

- If your home has a garden, it needs to be properly fenced as some kittens can jump higher than you might think.

- Put up a child gate to keep your kitten from going into rooms in your home that may hold toxic or dangerous items.

Kittens are known to chew and scratch almost everything they see. You will need to kitten-proof your home which means getting pretty much any item they can damage out of your kitten's way.

Getting your kitten settled

While it can be exciting for you to bring a new kitten home, your kitten will need some time to settle in. Your home is a new place for them, and they have just met you. It will take a bit of time for things to become familiar to your kitten. It is crucial to your kitten's well-being to help them settle into your home in their early days there. There have been many kittens given away because their owners could not handle them properly. Do your best to help your kitten be as comfortable and calm as possible.

Give your kitten their own space

It's a great idea to give your kitten some space that just belongs to them. Sort an area of your home that is only for them and will be where they will sleep. You can mark the area by putting down a chew-proof cat bed there along with some toys. Cats, especially kittens, need to have appropriate toys to help curb their chewing instinct. Keep in mind that they have smaller mouths as they are smaller cats. Place your kitten in the bed and give them a positive acknowledgment like "good kitty." You can also give them a little treat. Tell your kitten to "stay" and use a certain hand gesture like you are telling someone to halt. If your kitten stays, then reward them with another little treat. Incorporating hand gestures is helpful when your cat cannot hear you but can see you. It is good to get little bite-sized treats so as not to over-feed when teaching your kitten. These positive words and little treats are known as positive reinforcement.

Family meet & greet

When you bring your cat kitten home to meet the family make sure everyone is calm, and the kitten is not overwhelmed with everyone coming at the little darling all at once. Gentle introductions, one person at a time, are important. Each person can choose to stroke the kitten softly or let the kitten sniff their hands. Another good introduction is letting the kitten come up to people on its own. It is very important to teach children how to interact properly with the kitten. They should never pull the kitten's tail or come at the kitten from behind. It is vitally important that children are taught never to go near a kitten or cat when they are eating. Other behaviors, for children with kittens, that are a no-no are grabbing, poking, or lifting the cat up. It is good for cat kittens to be socialized with children and other adults from a young age to keep them more sociable. Be very careful picking up your cat. You need to remember that your kitten could scratch or bite you at any time. Do not let children rough-house with them or pick them up. Small children should not be left alone with cats as they may lash out at them.

Anxious kitten

Some kittens, when they are taken from their siblings and mother, get something called separation anxiety. Give your kitten some good attention and cuddles to give them assurance that all is well. There are also special collars containing pheromones that are used by cat charities to calm kittens and anxious cats when they are sent to new homes. The collars duplicate the pacification pheromone that is like the smell of the mother cat. The word CAP means 'cat appeasing pheromone' and additionally can be purchased and applied as a diffuser spray. Some people have found these effective in cats with separation anxiety or to prevent it when a cat or kitten goes to a new home.

Separation anxiety for kittens is, unsurprisingly, very common when they have been separated from their mother too soon. This can be due to an irresponsible breeder, or in the case of orphaned kittens. Kittens should not be parted from their mother and / or siblings until they are at least eight weeks old. Sometimes this is unavoidable, and the period can be a little shorter, but taking in a kitten less than eight weeks old means taking the risk of separation anxiety. Quite simply, your pet is too young to have been separated from its natural mother, brothers or sisters.

Another important, and related factor, is socialization. Being in the care of its natural family gives your kitten the time and space to learn to relate to other creatures. As cats are extremely sensitive, the smells, sounds, sights and feel of other animals, including people, are magnified in their developing brains. For this reason, best advice is that your kitten should be socialized between the ages of three and nine weeks. This means that, when you take your pet home, he or she will not be frightened of other animals, including human beings, be they young or old.

Helpful hint

To help keep your kitten from getting separation anxiety, make a point to not fuss over your kitten each and every single time you are near them. Don't praise them and give them eye contact and cuddles every time you see them or are near them. They will get used to this. If you make a big fuss over them every single time you see them, they can get stressed when you suddenly do not and have other things to do.

Kitten food

How you feed your kitten will very much depend on its age. A fully weaned kitten, after eight weeks old, should have no trouble eating twice a day, as would an adult cat. There is a wide choice of specially made kitten food on the market to help with this. If you take on a kitten younger than this, however, you will need to take extra care. Your seller or the shelter you get your pet from should be aware of its age, and what stage of weaning it's at. You should really consult your vet, as you may need to alternate between giving your kitten milk and feeding it solid food, at various times of the day. Feeding a new kitten from six weeks old is more easily manageable than for those younger than this age.

Kittens have a need to chew, especially when they are teething. Between three and six months old, your kitten will grow all of its adult teeth.

Helpful hint

It is best not to change what you feed your kitten often when they are young as it can upset their stomachs and possibly cause diarrhea. Kittens have sensitive stomachs in their early months. If, for any reason, you do need to change what they are eating it is best to do it slowly, adding a bit of the new food at a time.

Toys and chews

Kittens have a need to chew, especially when they are teething. Between three and six months old, your kitten will grow all of its adult teeth. Getting the proper toys for chewing is much better than ending up with your furniture or other belongings chewed to bits. There are many toys and chews on the market that are made especially for kittens. They are often made using catnip, which is a natural chemical found in plants. This will wear off after a few weeks of use.

- Catnip chew mice
- Fresh breath mint sticks
- Plaque removing pretzels
- Chewy wheels
- Stick shaped grinding toys
- Wiggle worm chews
- Supervising toys
- Purring cuddle pillows

As well as helping your kitten's teeth develop healthily, these chew toys will help with play, which is vital for any growing kitten. This will have the added bonus of giving you and your family some peace and quiet during this hectic stage of your kitten's young life.

House training your kitten

For such an adventurous, four-legged pet, house training a cat is remarkably easy, especially when compared to doing the same with a dog. Cats are naturally clean creatures, and it is in their nature to dispose of their own mess. In fact, as your cat grows up, you'll notice that things go missing. That could be because your cat has hidden them. A similar thing happens with its bodily waste.

In fact, cats prefer to go about their toilet business in private, which is a good first lesson for you as their owner to learn. Don't make the mistake of watching your kitten go to the toilet; give them their own space to do what's necessary. This will help both your kitten and you get over the relatively small hurdle of cat house training.

By the time you are able to take a kitten home, it will probably be house trained to some extent anyway. Kittens learn from watching their mothers; and by about eight weeks old, this process could be old hat to them. If your kitten is not fully house-trained, however, this shouldn't take long. As with everything else, getting used to new surroundings will be a large part of the battle.

Litter tray

Eventually, your kitten will go about its toilet business outside your home. To begin with, however, it may be necessary to help it with a litter tray, also called a litter box. Adult cats also use litter trays sometimes, so you should find a suitable spot to locate one. Adult cats scratch their litter after using it, so their trays need to have high sides, or even removable tops. For your kitten, however, the sides need to be low enough for them to climb in and out of easily.

Find a place for the litter tray which is away from open view, and is basically somewhere private. Think of it like this; you wouldn't want people watching you go to the toilet, and neither does your kitten. The litter box should also be well away from your kitten's feeding bowl. Choose a place for each, so your pet gets used to both locations early.

The litter tray should be far enough away from the feeding station so that your kitten can't smell it. You should also lay down some old newspapers under and around the tray, to catch litter which inevitably gets scratched aside.

It's really important to get your kitten acquainted with its litter tray as soon as you bring it home. Sit your new pet directly in the litter straight away, and give it time to remember the place and feel of the tray. Once settled into your home, put your kitten in its tray just before bed, and first thing in the morning. You'll find your kitten likes to use the toilet at both these times of day. Also, lift your kitten to its tray directly after every meal. This will help it associate using the toilet to after having eaten.

It's important to keep an eye on your kitten in its early stages, and using the toilet is a very good reason for this. If you notice your kitten scratching and or sniffing around for nothing in particular, this could be a sign that it needs to go to the toilet. An especially clear sign of this is if it starts to crouch, as it would when evacuating. If you notice any of these signs, lift your kitten into its tray immediately. If your kitten uses the tray correctly, praise it afterwards. If not, however, don't raise your voice and scold your pet. This will only make it nervous about its own natural bodily functions.

There is an old myth that the way to teach an animal not to defecate in a particular spot is by rubbing its nose in it. This is a terrible idea for kittens, who will already be distressed about leaving a mess. Make it clear you're pleased when things go as you'd like, but don't make things worse when they go slightly wrong. If your kitten does have an accident of this kind, just place it in its tray and leave it in peace. You can then clean up the mess so that your kitten can't smell it.

Helpful hint

Be careful not to use ammonia, as this smells similar to cat urine to a kitten.

Kitty Litter

In terms of the litter itself, you have a wide range of choice. The basic point of cat litter is to absorb urine, and disguise feces. There are litters on the market which have built in deodorizers, which helps disguise the smells of both. Remember, your cat has an extremely acute sense of smell, and doesn't like to go anywhere dirty.

With this in mind, you should change your kitten's litter once a day, if it has been used. If you notice any feces, remove them straight away and dispose of them appropriately. You should clean your kitten's litter tray completely once a week, emptying the litter and washing out the tray itself. If you choose to use disinfectant, be careful not to use one which contains phenol, as this is poisonous for your kitten. Also, strong-smelling disinfectant products could put off your kitten from using its tray. After you've finished, remember to wash your hands thoroughly to get rid of any disinfectant smell.

Training problems

If your kitten does experience problems when learning to use its litter tray, don't worry; you can fix this, with time and patience. Problems do occur, as accidents will happen. Your kitten may have a bout of diarrhea, for example, which means it can't get to its tray in time. Or it could be something as simple as an unexpected event which throws your everyday routine with your kitten out of step. If your pet accidentally soils an area it shouldn't, you should take prompt action to help prevent this happening again.

If your kitten does experience problems when learning to use its litter tray, don't worry; you can fix this, with time and patience.

Training Help

- Keep your kitten's litter and litter tray clean at all times, so it doesn't put your pet off using it properly.

- Take care with smells, such as disinfectant or particular types of litter. You may find that changing to a new brand of litter solves the problem.

- Make your kitten's tray as accessible and private as possible. The sides should be easy to climb over, and the try should be well out of human sight.

- If your kitten repeatedly soils one area, try putting its feeding bowl nearby. This will make it less likely to repeat the behavior.

- If you catch your kitten during the act of soiling, spray it with water from a bottle spray container, or even a water pistol. This will surprise it, without doing it any harm. Remember, cats have excellent memories.

- If your kitten continues to soil inappropriate areas, you should take it to the veterinarian. There could be a medical reason for its behavior.

Going outdoors

As your kitten grows up, it will want to explore the outside world. This is perfectly natural behavior for all cats, who set up their own zones around their home base. The process of house training your kitten and letting it outside is one that needs to be done carefully, however. If you let your kitten out and about too soon, it could easily come to harm. Keep it inside for too long, on the other hand, and you risk making your kitten frightened of the outside world.

Your new kitten will need a couple of weeks to get used to its new surroundings, inside its home. This period should also see it well able to use its litter tray, and feed regularly. Also, and very importantly, this time will allow your kitten's vaccinations to do their job. You mustn't let your kitten outdoors until the allotted period has elapsed for vaccinations to take effect. Your vet will advise you on this. Once you do decide to give your kitten room to roam outdoors, it may be worth keeping it in a confined area, so it cannot escape, and is not in danger from other cats, or any other animals in the area.

For most cat owners, a cat flap is an absolute necessity. These can be locked shut when your kitten is very young, so it can't get out unless you're there to supervise it. When you think it's ready for the big, wide world, introduce your kitten to its very own doorway. To start with, you could keep the flap in an open position, and encourage your kitten to step through it, both into and out of your home. Once it's got the hang of this, let the flap close as it is designed to do. It won't take your kitten long to use its paw to try to open it. After that, there's no looking back. You can still lock the flap shut at nights, as long as you're sure your kitten's indoors.

Spraying

Cats are territorial animals, and use scent to mark out their patch. While this is natural behavior, it can cause problems for owners. Once your kitten has access to the outdoors, it will urinate in various places to mark its territory. Again, this goes back to cats' reliance on their sense of smell. Cat territories form invisible areas of land which humans know nothing about. This is especially true when your kitten grows into adolescence. Once it becomes sexually active, you may have to have your cat neutered. Watching out for signs of spraying behavior is a good way to keep an eye on your kitten's development. If you have more than one kitten, or adult cats, in your home, they may fall into disputes over territory.

Your kitten and teething

Your kitten will probably have some of its primary, or deciduous, teeth when you first take him or her home with you for the first time. As cats' teeth are extremely sharp, they don't erupt until part of the way through weaning, to avoid injuring their mother. By about eight weeks of age, which is when you'll probably take in your kitten, the process of teething will have started. For this reason, you should take care of your kitten's gums as soon as you get it home. Just as teeth are painful for mothers, so they are painful when erupting through your kitten's gums.

Your kitten will eventually have 26 "baby" teeth, which will start appearing from about three weeks old. You should brush your kitten's gums and what teeth they have straight away. Your vet will give you the best advice as to how and when to do this, and what products to use. Bear in mind that, as teeth erupt, your kitten may sometimes not be keen on eating, will probably drool, and / or may chew with one side of its mouth. On the other hand, after the initial painful breakthrough, your kitten will try to chew anything and everything it can.

Once all 26 of your kitten's deciduous teeth are present, the teething process doesn't stop. At about 3½ to 4 months, its adult teeth will start to come through. These will push the baby teeth out of the mouth, which will grow during the process. When your kitten is between six and seven months old, it should have all its adult teeth. There are 30 of these; 4 more than 'baby' teeth. While these adult teeth are erupting, your kitten will again want to chew anything it can get hold of. As it will now be older and stronger, you'll have to make sure it can't get its claws and teeth into clothing, shoes or expensive furniture. Your kitten's breath may also smell rather bad at certain times during the teething process. This is natural, as the old teeth have outlived their usefulness.

Sometimes, deciduous teeth get retained by kittens. This means their roots to not get fully re-absorbed, which they would in the normal way of things. As the adult teeth continue to grow and push outwards, this can cause problems for your kitten. As teeth are jostling for position, your kitten's bit might become uneven, leading to problems chewing. More serious is the issue of infection, which can happen if deciduous roots are only partly re-absorbed. If you notice any problems with your kitten retaining its baby teeth, you should take it to your vet without delay. It could be that surgery is required, which should be carried out as soon as possible.

Vaccines

Having your kitten vaccinated isn't compulsory, but is something any responsible cat owner should do anyway. Rather than take the risk, you can keep your new pet as safe as possible from diseases which are known to affect young cats. Just as you would have your child vaccinated against common diseases, so you should with your kitten. Also, good catteries will insist that your pet is vaccinated before they will accept them as boarders, as will any pet travel insurance provider. Apart from all that, of course, you are cutting out any chance of your kitten developing what could be very distressing and possibly fatal diseases.

Kitten vaccinations are available for what are called core and non-core protection. Obviously, core vaccinations are considered the more important, and are recommended for cats of all breeds and circumstances. These are;

> Having your kitten vaccinated isn't compulsory, but is something any responsible cat owner should do anyway. Rather than take the risk, you can keep your new pet as safe as possible from diseases which are known to affect young cats.

Core Vaccinations

- **Feline Panleukopenia Virus (FPV).** This is a highly contagious virus which can be fatal for young kittens. It attacks their underdeveloped digestive tracts, which are vulnerable in the first few weeks of life. Symptoms of FPV include vomiting, diarrhea and fever. Severe dehydration takes place very quickly, which could lead to your kitten feeling very thirsty, while not wanting or able to eat. The fever could also lead to nervous excitement, as the brain overheats.

- **Feline Calicivirus.** This is also called "cat 'flu", and is particularly distressing for kittens. Symptoms include drooling, mouth ulcers, nasal discharge and sneezing. Your kitten will also have no appetite, and a high temperature.

- **Feline Herpesvirus.** This also has 'flu like symptoms, such as nasal discharge and sneezing, and may result in ulcers on both the eyes and mouth. As herpes is a recurrent virus, exposure to it can lead to permanent nasal problems for your cat in later years.

Non-core vaccinations will depend on a number of factors, but you may want to consider them if you are thinking of breeding your cat in future, or if you want to take your kitten overseas with you. Typical non-core vaccinations are;

Non-Core Vaccinations

- Feline Leukaemia Virus (FLV); this is spread by contact with other cats or possibly other animals, and can lead to blood disorders including cancer, as well as anemia, diarrhea and vomiting.

- Rabies. This is essential when taking your cat abroad. Your vet may advise you to have your kitten vaccinated against rabies at an early age.

Core vaccinations are best given as soon as you take your kitten home, from about eight weeks of age. They will then be supplemented with boosters as your kitten becomes an adult cat. Initial vaccinations need two injections, about three to four weeks apart. Again, consult with your vet for the best advice. Vaccinations do not mean your kitten is 100% protected from disease, but they will have a much better chance of surviving them, especially at a young and vulnerable age. Also, bear in mind that vaccinations can take a couple of weeks to take full effect, as your kitten's immune system adapts to cope.

Worms and fleas

Your kitten is likely to have worms at some point in its life. It might not sound nice, but worms are very common in the animal kingdom. In fact, your kitten may already have worms when you first take it home, as they can get passed down through their mothers' milk. These are roundworm larvae, which are small enough to find their way into the mother's reproductive system. These are then ingested by the kitten, and take root in its intestines, which is where they attach and grow to maturity. Roundworm larvae are also expelled by infected cats when they defecate. These then disperse into surrounding soil or other ground material, making them easy for other animals to lick or otherwise re-ingest.

The flatworm is another common type of worm infestation suffered by cats and kittens. Flatworm larvae are present in the guts of infected fleas, which attach themselves to cats' fur at the base. When your kitten grooms itself, it dislodges and sometimes eats these fleas. By doing so, it also eats the flatworm larvae, which can then find their way into the wall of your kitten's gut. As your kitten grows, it will also start to hunt bigger creatures than fleas; any of these it catches and eats could be infected with flatworm larvae. Luckily, both roundworm and flatworm can be treated easily and effectively with modern procedures and products. Ask your vet about worming; and take action as soon as possible. Treated correctly, there is no reason your kitten should suffer unduly due to worm infestation.

More about vet visits

Your vet will check your cat's heart, teeth, coat, temperature, ears, and eyes during a check-up. They will also keep track of your kitten's weight to see if they are growing properly. Vets should go out of their way to make this as good of an experience as possible for your kitten.

3

The Cat Teenager

As your kitten becomes a teenager, you will have different matters to deal with. Will you have your cat spayed or neutered? Will you invest in micro-chipping your cat? Will you make sure to socialise your cat with other cats to keep them well-rounded? What happens if they get loose and go walk-about while you are taking them out on a walk?

Spay or neuter?

When your cat is of age to reproduce it is a good time to think about getting them neutered or spayed. Some cat owners feel that it is unnatural to spay or neuter their pet. Other owners, like breeders, want their cat to have kittens. Unless you are a professional breeder with specific knowledge, you may not know your way around which cats should be bred with which. Breeders usually match particular cats for particular traits. The most widespread view is that it is a much healthier choice to neuter or spay cats.

Reasons for spay/neuter

- If you spay your female cat, they will not have to experience being on heat. When a female is on heat, usually she will need to be confined to the home and garden to avoid them falling pregnant.

- Spaying your female cat can lower their chances of getting urinary issues, ovarian disease, and some cancers.

- With male cats, spraying can be unpleasant, especially for families with young children. Quite simply, the smell of a mature, unspayed cat's urine is extremely pungent. Mature males also get very territorial and aggressive with other cats, which can lead to them getting injured.

- Most experts will agree that it is healthier for your cat to be spayed or neutered.

The cons of spay/neuter

- For breeders, spay and neuter is a con as they will not be able to breed new cats.

- Spay/neuter is not an inexpensive operation. However, some animal rescues offer vouchers for discounts.

- Spayed/neutered cats can put on more weight. If you feed your cat a healthy diet this can be cured. Ask your vet how much food they recommend for your cat.

- Some people worry about their cat being put under anesthetic for the surgery. Anesthetics these days are much better than they used to be and usually, the benefit of spay/neuter outweighs the risk of the surgery.

Unsettling news

Thousands of cats and kittens are dropped off at charities like Cats Trust and the RSPCA every year. Many times, it is because their owners cannot properly take care of them or because they no longer want the responsibility. This problem is magnified by the fact that there are so many unwanted kittens born due to lack of spay and neuter. Many animal charities, local authorities, and vets offer discounted or free spay or neuter for cats to help prevent this problem.

Most vets usually agree that male cats can be neutered at any age, as the procedure is safe. Usually, the operation is carried out at the age of between four and six months.

What is the recommended age for spay/neuter surgery?

Most vets usually agree that male cats can be neutered at any age, as the procedure is safe. Usually, the operation is carried out at the age of between four and six months. This is when your kitten reaches sexual maturity.

How does spay/neuter surgery work?

- The reproductive organs of female cats are removed in spay surgery; sometimes both the ovaries and the uterus, but sometimes just the ovaries. The testicles of male cats are removed in neuter surgery.

- The night before the surgery your cat will not be able to eat after a certain time as they want your cat to be on an empty stomach for the surgery for safety reasons. It is important to follow the vet's instructions as to when is the latest you can feed your cat the night before.

- Your cat will need a check-up at the vet before their surgery to make sure they are fit for the operation. While the operation is being performed, your cat's vital signs will be watched. Depending on the time of the surgery, your cat may need to stay overnight.

- Your cat should not be in a lot of pain after the surgery. Males tend to bounce back much more quickly than females. There will be some discomfort. Your cat will want to lick the wound. Try to get them not to. Some vets will give you a cone to put around their neck to avoid licking. If anything seems off, call your vet right away. It is better to be safe than sorry.

- Cats take fourteen days to recover from neutering surgery. During this time, they will be vulnerable to infection and injury. They will also be in pain for the first few days.

Keep an eye out for the following:

- If your cat is still lethargic after a couple of days, call your vet for advice.

- If the incision turns a nasty shade of purple or red, if it starts to open, or if anything oozes out of it contact your vet right away.

- The incision area may swell some. If you feel it is severely swollen, then contact your vet right away.

Is spay/neuter surgery safe?

These surgeries are routinely done every day. For the most part, they are very safe. However, with any use of anesthesia or surgery, there is a tiny risk that things can happen. Spay and neuter procedures are routine for vets, and they do them a lot. So, your vet would be very experienced if anything were to happen. Speak with your vet about any questions you may have.

When can I breed my cat?

You need to ask yourself if you can make sure that each kitten you breed will find a good home. If you cannot guarantee that, then it might not be a good idea to breed your cat. A litter of kittens sounds like a fun thing, but it is a lot of work keeping up with them. You have to clean their mess, keep an eye on their health, make sure they get wormed and have vaccinations. It is a costly endeavor both time-wise and financially. Think twice and do your research before attempting to breed your cat.

Why microchip my cat?

Microchipping is highly recommended by cat charities as it is a safe way to reunite lost cats with their owners. Some reasons for this are:

- Microchipping works to reduce the number of stray cats. When a stray cat is taken in by a cat warden, vet or charity it is checked immediately for a microchip. If the information on the chip is up to date, the cat can be returned to its owner.

- Microchipping your cat ensures that you can prove you are the rightful owner. This is especially important if someone steals your cat and claims it is theirs. Microchipping helps reduce cat theft

- It is relatively cheap to microchip and register your cat. Some groups even hold events for free microchipping. The RSPCA has done such events in the past.

4

Dangerous Foods for your Cat

There are many dangerous items for cats in your home if they are eaten by your cat. We will go over some of those and what you should do if your cat eats some of the banned list items.

Chocolate – the biggest no-no

One of the most dangerous foods for cats is chocolate. Most cats will have a bad reaction to eating chocolate, and it is not worth the risk giving it to your beloved cat. There is a compound called theobromine in chocolate that is made for humans. It can kill cats even in smaller doses. There is a special chocolate for cats in supermarkets and pet stores that does not contain this compound. However, this can be confusing if you have children in the home who may not understand the difference.

If my cat has chocolate what should I do?

Don't panic if your cat eats chocolate. The poisoning caused by chocolate in cats is usually built up over time. If your cat just had a small amount, they should be ok. However, you should always call your vet for advice to be on the safe side. If your cat has eaten a lot of chocolate, then rush them to the vet immediately, calling ahead to let them know you are coming. If your cat gets medical care quickly enough then hopefully their life will be spared.

What does chocolate poisoning look like?

A cat that has been poisoned by chocolate will usually have diarrhea and vomit. You may see chocolate in the vomit. Your cats may be even more hyper than usual, and if you touch their stomach, they will react as if in pain. As the poisoning goes on, they may have issues with walking and may shake and twitch. Some cats even have convulsions. It may take hours after your cat has eaten the chocolate for them to get these symptoms as chocolate can take a while to digest.

How to treat chocolate poisoning

If your cat has not already vomited, their veterinarian may give them something to make them vomit. If they have been vomiting repeatedly then they will be given a drug to stop the vomiting. Your vet will next give your cat something like charcoal to absorb the poison. Intravenous fluids will be administered to keep your cat from getting dehydrated. Unfortunately, chocolate is not the only food item that cats should not eat. There are other kinds.

Coffee and tea

Caffeine is not good for cats, and it can cause a poisoning like chocolate does.

Onions and garlic

Onions can cause anemia in cats due to a toxic chemical they contain and can cause breathing issues with your cat.

Milk

Cats can be lactose intolerant just like humans. Some symptoms of this are when they have smelly farts or their stomach bloats. It's best not to feed your cat milk, especially if they have these symptoms.

Cheese

Cheese should not be given to cats in large amounts. It can give them diarrhea and give them issues with their pancreas.

Sultanas, raisins, and grapes

A majority of cats cannot digest sultanas, grapes, and raisins. If they eat them, they can have renal failure. There have been cats who have ended up dead after eating just a few grapes.

Raw meat, fish eggs and fat trimmings

Any of these can cause diarrhea, and possibly pancreatitis if your cat eats excessive amounts of fat. There is also the risk of salmonella poisoning from raw meat and eggs.

Alcohol

Your cat's heart and central nervous system can be affected by alcohol. In some cases, alcohol has killed cats. Keep alcohol away from your cat.

Xylitol

It has been found out that a sweetener called Xylitol that is found in many sugar-free food items like biscuits, mints and chewing gum is toxic to cats. This sweetener is found in sugar-free foodstuffs, like chewing gum and biscuits

Other items to keep away from your cat:

- Human medicines- keep them locked away up high!

- Rat poison and anti-freeze

- Weed-killer (do not put weed-killer down on your grass if your cat is likely to eat the grass!)

- Human vitamin supplements

If your cat has any of these call your vet's emergency number right away. Keep hydrogen peroxide 3% around as it can be used to induce vomiting if your vet recommends that. Bring the bottle of whatever your cat has ingested to the vet with you. Even if your cat looks fine, get them to a vet right away if they have had any of these bullet-pointed items.

Bring the bottle of whatever your cat has ingested to the vet with you. Even if your cat looks fine, get them to a vet right away if they have had any of these items.

5

First Aid for your Cat

If your cat falls ill or suffers injuries of any kind, it may fall to you to treat them. As cats are very self-sufficient, making an intervention will probably be very unusual. Both you and your cat may find the experience somewhat traumatic. While your cat will live its life regardless in the meantime, you should keep at the back of your mind that you may have to help it one day. This preparedness can be as vital as any medical expertise.

Of course, you are not expected to do everything yourself. In most situations, the vet will be the person to properly fix or remedy your cat's injury or illness, however minor. With that in mind, the following should be of comfort in any situation:

A Vet's Obligation

Legally, all veterinary surgeons are obliged to treat any cat, even if it does not belong to their client. All vets must offer an out of hours contact for emergencies. To find a vet in an emergency there are several resources:

Your local listings publications, such as yellow pages;

Any local generic telephone help number, other than the emergency services;

www.any-uk-vet.co.uk

The Royal College of Veterinary Surgeons Website (RCVS)

https://findavet.rcvs.org.uk/home/

Try to always use the number listed instead of one saved in your phone in case the contact number for emergencies has changed. **Always have your vet's number handy.**

Safety First

It may not always be possible to help your cat. While this might not seem like a positive way to prepare, it should be borne in mind. There may be situations where doing nothing might be the best course of action. It is important to take a breath and consider the consequences of any actions you might take. Rushing in might not be the right way to prove you love your cat.

Think about the following things:

- Will you put your own safety at risk? You are no help to your cat if you yourself get injured, even temporarily. Although cats are resourceful, you are your pet's main source of food and shelter. Ask yourself if there is a likelihood you will suffer injury, say from passing traffic, being swept away by water or even drowning.

- Will your added presence to the situation put your cat or other people at increased risk? Ask yourself whether standing back and offering to help might be a better solution.

- Do you need to call the emergency services? While it might be tempting to think about your cat first, there might be a situation which requires attention immediately. Obvious examples are a road traffic collision, railway accident or burning building. Ask yourself if the emergency services shouldn't be involved as soon as possible.

- Are you ready to take action? Your cat may be in severe pain, which will make it want to strike out and dig its claws into you. You may have to take control of your cat by physical means you would never use otherwise. Ask yourself if you feel ready to overcome your own squeamishness.

By taking these things into consideration, you have already taken the first step in helping your cat, whether he or she is injured or feeling ill. Remember, a cornered cat is not a happy animal. All its instincts will be to get away from its current situation, of which you will be a major part. When it comes to these situations, all bets are off. You may have to overcome the feeling that you are your cat's worst enemy.

First Aid Kit

As being prepared to take the right action is a vital part of giving first aid to your cat, you will find it a great help to have a first aid kit ready. By itemizing what is in it, and how to use everything, you should feel more confident if and when the time comes to give first aid. This in turn will help you keep calm and make the right choices. The quicker you take any action, the better.

Cat First Aid Kit

With a good first aid kit, you will be best placed to take the first steps in getting your cat better. Whether this is just in preparation for a visit to the vet, or a permanent solution, the right tools are a great help. Here are the basics of what you should have at hand, and be confident in using:

- a roll of self-adhesive or crepe bandages (5cm width)
- conforming / open-weave bandages (2.5cm width)
- non-adhesive absorbent dressings (5cm x 5cm) to cover open wounds

- surgical sticky tape
- a box of cotton wool
- a box of sterile absorbent gauze
- blunt ended scissors, preferably curved
- a thick towel
- rectal thermometer

- foil blanket
- disposable, sterile gloves
- saline eye or wound washes
- tweezers
- washing soda crystals
- an Elizabethan collar

Elizabethan Collars

An Elizabethan collar has many names, including buster collar, pet cone and E-collar. Light-hearted names include pet lamp-shade and pet radar dish. These collars may look strange, but they prevent your cat from doing what it does naturally – licking its paws to clean its face. As these collars protect the head, this means your cat won't be able to access its own eyes, ears, nose or mouth. If any of these areas is infected or injured, it's vital that they are left alone once treated.

Although your cat will not like wearing one, practice putting one on while it's healthy and contented. This may give you some idea of the challenges you'll face when the time comes to do it for real. Depending on the temperament of your cat, these could be quite considerable. Of course, your cat won't thank you for it, but at least you'll be prepared.

What to do in an Emergency

If, after thinking "Safety First" (see above), you decide it is safe to make a positive intervention, there are some situations where prompt and effective action can be vital to save your cat.

On no account give your cat any medicine designed for human consumption. If you are taking your cat to the veterinary surgeon, do not give it food or water, in case it might need general anesthetic.

On no account give your cat any medicine designed for human consumption. If you are taking your cat to the veterinary surgeon, do not give it food or water, in case it might need general anesthetic.

Describe the situation exactly

When calling the vet in an emergency situation, it is essential you think clearly. They will want to know exactly what is happening, and why you called them. Bearing in mind this may not be your usual vet, describing the details of the situation and your cat's symptoms precisely can be life-saving. The vet will want to know:

- What type of problem your cat has, and how severe it is. They will ask if your cat has stopped breathing, or if it has difficulty breathing, how the breaths are coming. The vet will also ask if your cat is bleeding, and if so, how heavily and where from. They might also ask if you suspect your cat has taken poison of some sort, and if so, why you think so.

- How long the problem has been happening. If your cat is showing signs of illness, the vet will want to assess how persistent the illness is. For instance, if it has severe diarrhea, how often is it, and since when? Also, if you suspect your cat has been poisoned, when was the last time you saw it eat or drink something which might be the cause.

- Exact details about your cat. While some of the vet's questions might seem irrelevant or confusing, they will have good reasons for asking them. Remember, you are talking to the professionals, who will know more about your cat than you do in many ways. Keep a clear head, and remember your cat's breed, sex, weight, age, medical history, any medication it takes and possibly what you feed it. A vet might be able to identify a possible cause of illness very quickly based on their knowledge and experience. This can make treatment much quicker to affect.

Accidents And Severe Onset Illness

If your cat is involved in accidents or mishaps, or becomes trapped in dangerous situations, it will obviously need help as soon as possible. As long as you are in a position to do so, call an emergency vet without delay in the following situations:

- Road traffic accidents, especially when a wheel or wheels goes over any body part
- Penetrating eye or throat injuries
- Impact with your cat's head
- Obvious ingestion of anything toxic
- Overheating or hypothermia.

Symptoms Which May Need Quick Action

As cats can be good at hiding their injuries, being vigilant when they come home is always a good idea. Any change in behavior could signal something is wrong. If your cat usually dashes from the cat flap to its dinner bowl, but doesn't one time, ask yourself why? This will be a natural reaction on your part anyway, so back this up by finding your cat if you can.

Signs to Look Out For

There are other signs which your cat will not be able to hide from you. Have a look out for these:

- Difficulty breathing
- Panting
- Drooling
- Abdominal heaving
- Bleeding
- Foaming at the mouth
- Seizures or muscle spasms
- Persistent vomiting and / or diarrhea
- Straining when urinating
- Blood in the urine

- Crying when urinating
- Urinating in unusual places
- Licking the urinary area
- Depression
- Lack of appetite
- Lameness
- Weight loss
- Fever
- Dark or bloody stools
- Sunken eyes

- Lethargy
- Dry mouth
- Elevated heart rate
- Decreased skin elasticity
- Squinting
- Pawing the eye / eyes
- Visible third eyelid
- Watery discharge from eye / eyes
- Red, inflamed eyes
- Sticky or yellow eye discharge

Some emergencies affecting your cat are more urgent than others; this doesn't mean they should be given less importance. Of course, heavy bleeding and / or difficulty breathing will be more immediately worrying. Other symptoms may not require immediate attention, but remember your cat could be in pain or distress of some kind.

If you do have an immediate emergency, it is vital to stay as calm as possible. This will help you keep a clear head, to ask yourself the questions which could lead to a correct diagnosis. If you can't manage this, panicking will only make things worse. Even if you only manage to remember where your vet's number is, any time you save could be of great importance.

Cat First Aid Basics

Giving first aid to any living creature is something which benefits from practice. There are physical and emotional barriers to overcome, something which is best done as quickly as possible. If you can, attend a pet first aid course hosted by an accredited pet care organization. This will give you practical tips based on the experience of other cat owners and veterinary professionals. Unless you've ever given first aid to your cat, or another animal, it's hard to know where to start. This can lead to hesitation and mistakes when action is needed most. Nervousness on your part could do your cat more harm than good.

Familiarity can be extremely important in situations where pain and fear are involved, and especially so with cats. A cat's first instinct when injured or ill may be to attack anything or anyone that comes near it. As a cat owner, hopefully you should have experience of what to expect when approaching your pet. This will guide you as to any precautions you think you should take. Always remember, only attempt first aid if you judge it safe to do so.

With that in mind, here are some things to take on board.

Pay Attention

As cats are usually shy creatures, they can be hard to read. Changes in behavior can be subtle, and very easy to miss if you're not paying attention. What might be easier to spot is erratic behavior. Cats are often creatures of habit, even if not necessarily at the same time every day. If you notice your cat not doing its usual rounds, for instance, this could be something to watch out for. Cats can suffer from depression or even dehydration, which knocks them off their usual rhythm.

Cats do try to communicate with humans, even if it is not so obvious as with other pets. Your cat will certainly let you know when it's hungry, of course. It will also let you know when it's content, in a number of ways, some of them much more subtle than lying on you and purring. For a cat, doing nothing in particular can be a sign that all is well. Doing nothing at all, over a period of days, however, is different. This could be a sign of many a hidden illness, some of which cats are, unfortunately, prone to. We'll see some of them later in this guide.

Of course, the better you know your cat, the easier the signs will be to spot that something is wrong. It may just be a tick, for example, which is easily removed if you have your tick remover with you. The point is, the sooner you spot any danger signs, the better position you are in to do something about it.

Call the Vet First

Before you take any action yourself, call your vet. Even if your usual vet is not there in person, someone will be able to assist you. Don't act without asking advice first. Your veterinary surgery may advise you not to do anything and wait for someone to come to you. Alternatively, they may advise you to take your cat to them yourself, if you have suitable means of doing so safely.

Calming and Preparing Your Cat

If your cat has suffered a distressing injury, or is feeling particularly unwell, you may need to stabilize it. As cats are very sensitive creatures, they can become upset easily. This can lead to further injury or worse illness, as the cat panics because of something it doesn't understand.

Even if you are able to deal with the problem yourself, you will find that having techniques to calm and stabilize your cat come in extremely useful. If, on the other hand, you need to wait for, or travel to, a vet, keeping your cat stable can be absolutely vital to its overall health and well-being.

1 **Protection.** Wear long sleeved and legged clothing. Your cat may try to bite and or scratch you. Also, carry a thick towel, in case you need to grab your pet. Approach with extreme caution, slowly and deliberately.

2 **Preparation.** Calm your cat using any and all methods you can think of. Normality is calming, for instance; put the television or radio on, as you would normally. Sing softly, especially if this is something you normally do around your cat. Talk to it calmly, letting it know every thing's all right. Sit down and be patient.

3 **Enticement.** Once your cat is somewhat calmer, offer it some food. As cats prefer wet food rather than dry, open some of this. If you have some fishy food handy, use that. Cats love the smell of fish, which takes their mind off just about everything else that's going on. Once your cat accepts the food, stroke it gently with your thumb, from its nose upwards.

4 Isolation. If none of the above calms your cat to a point where you can approach it, the best thing will be to isolate it. This will be its natural instinct anyway, so it will cooperate with you if you help it work with you.

You can do this by leaving it in the room it's already in, and removing distractions one by one. Get everyone out of the room, turn everything off, and close the curtains. Then back out of the room and close the door.

If you want to take your cat into another room, you should do this carefully. Find and prepare a small room first, which is quiet and dark. Approach your cat as detailed above, using your towel, pick it up and cradle it so just its head is visible. Talking to it calmly, carry it into the quiet room, lay it down and back out, closing the door behind you.

Once your cat is safely calmed down, and depending on the situation as outlined above, you may be able to apply first aid yourself, if your vet has advised it. Otherwise, your cat is able to be calmly transported to the veterinary surgery.

Spray your cat's carrier with a synthetic pheromone cat scent, at least 15 minutes before using it. If you know that your cat will panic when it sees the carrier, put it close by, but out of sight.

Choking

Choking is one of the most worrying things that can happen to your cat. It will be extremely distressed and frightened, and no doubt so will you. It is, of course, vital not to panic in such a situation. You will need a very calm head in order to act quickly to remove the obstacle. Depending on how long the choking has been happening, you might then need to resuscitate your cat. Both of these steps can be achieved with the right knowledge and attitude on your behalf.

> **If your cat is showing signs of choking, you will first need to restrain it. As it will already be in a state of panic, any attempt on your part to access its throat will cause it to want to bite you.**

If your cat is showing signs of choking, you will first need to restrain it. As it will already be in a state of panic, any attempt on your part to access its throat will cause it to want to bite you. In other situations, your cat might actually be unconscious. If this is the case, the procedure is slightly different.

What to Look Out For

If your cat is choking, it has something stuck in its larynx or trachea. If this is the case, these are the signs to look for:

need2know

- Anxiety or panic

- Bad breath, loss of appetite, or listlessness

- Coughing or gagging

- Fainting, unconsciousness, or inability to breathe

- Labored breathing

- Pawing at the mouth, and / or drooling.

Gaining Access

If you have calmed and restrained your cat, or if it is unconscious, its mouth may be shut. To open it, take hold of its upper jaw with your fingers and thumb. This is the safest way of ensuring your cat is not able to bite you, whether it is conscious or not. If it is unconscious and wakes up suddenly, its first instinct may well be to bite.

- Open your cat's mouth fully with your other hand. Pull its tongue forward and down, and have a look deep into the back of its mouth. If you can see what is causing the blockage.

- If you can see an object in your cat's throat, take the tweezers from the first aid kid and try to take hold of it. If you get a decent grip, try to pull it forwards out of your cat's mouth.

- If the obstruction is a piece of bone, this is hard to do. Don't spend too long trying to remove any object if you can't get a decent grip. It's more important to take your cat to the vet as soon as possible.

If you can't see any obstruction, your next step should be the Heimlich Maneuver. This is something you should practice on a Pet First Aid course as soon as you get the chance.

- Lie your cat on its side. Put the flat of one hand along the length of its back.

- Place the flat of your other hand on your cat's abdomen, just below the rib cage. Put the heel of your hand furthest away from its head, with your fingers facing that way.

- With one hand steady against your cat's spine, push the heel of your other hand sharply into its belly, below the ribs. Do this a few times, quickly.

- Check your cat's mouth, to see if there are any foreign objects in it which have been dislodged by your attempts. If there is anything there, pull it away.

- Close your cat's mouth and breathe into its nose a couple of times.

- Repeat this whole process until you are sure there is nothing left obstructing your cat's throat.

- If you cannot dislodge the choking object from your cat's throat, take it to a vet immediately. See our section on *Transporting Your cat Safely*.

If you do manage to dislodge the object, your cat may start breathing again spontaneously. If it does not, you'll need to resuscitate it.

Resuscitation

One of the most important things you may ever be able to do for your cat is resuscitate it. While this process is something mostly associated with people, in fact it is perfectly possible to carry out on your pet. Acting quickly and appropriately in the right circumstances can quite simply save your cat's life. Of course, no cat owner ever wants to be put in such a situation. If you are, however, it is helpful to remember that the successful steps to resuscitation are literally A, B, C. This stands for Airway, Breathing and Circulation.

ABC and CPR

Another handy acronym to remember when thinking about resuscitating your cat is CPR. This stands for Cardio Pulmonary Resuscitation, and works on exactly the same principles as with humans. Basically, if your cat is in serious trouble and has stopped breathing, you can resuscitate it by getting its heart and lungs working properly again. The quicker you are able to do this, as with humans, the less damage is likely to have been done. As long as your pet's brain has not been starved of oxygen for too long, a complete recovery is possible.

Of course, you need to be confident when attempting CPR on your cat. There are classes available which will show you what to look for, and what procedures to carry out. These use feline CPR manikins, which are specially designed to give you an idea of what it feels like to resuscitate your cat.

What manikins cannot replicate, however, is the smell of your cat's breath. Like the shape of its whiskers, you will no doubt be familiar with this. It is details such as these which can tell you if your cat is need of resuscitation.

Airway

If your cat is immobile and you cannot rouse it, there is obviously something wrong. In order to check to see if it's breathing, you can look for its rib cage. If you feel or see no movement there, check its nose. You will be able to see any signs of breath on its whiskers. If these are still, put your face close to your cat's mouth and nose. You will be able to detect the smell of its breath if it is breathing.

If none of these signs are present, open your cat's mouth gently. Pull its tongue forward out of the way and check inside for any objects in its throat. If you see something, try and remove it with tweezers. Do not push any obstructions further down your cat's throat. Pull the tongue all the way out in order to help any object free itself.

Once any obstructions are out of the way, your cat may start to breathe. If it does not, and you are sure there are no obstructions in its throat, you should check for a heartbeat. To do this, put your finger tips under your cat's left leg where it joins its body. You will feel any heart beat through gaps in its ribs. If you feel nothing, you need to start resuscitation quickly.

Breathing

With your cat on its side, lift its nose upwards slightly so that its head tilts backward enough to open its airway completely. Once you've done this, pull your cat's tongue to the front of its mouth, just behind its teeth. With the tongue in that position, gently close your cat's mouth, and hold it shut.

- Making sure your cat's neck is straight, in line with its spine, breath into your cat's nose, once every four to five seconds. As you'll have your lips pursed, you won't be able to blow too much air into your cat's lungs, so don't worry about that. Do this three to five times, then check your cat for a heartbeat and / or breathing.

- If there is still no sign of either, repeat the above, with one breath every six seconds, or ten a minute. You will need someone to drive you and your cat to the vet while you are doing this.

Circulation

If your cat's heart stops, you will need to get it started again. To help get your cat's heart beating, combine breathing with compression. In between breaths, compress your cat's rib cage enough to press on its heart.

- Lay your cat on its side, preferably on a hard, flat surface. This should also be far enough from the ground to give you reasonable access to it without bending all the way down every time. This treatment may last quite a long time.

- Using just one hand, put your thumb on one side, and fingers on the other, of its rib cage You should do this just behind your cat's elbows, where its front legs join its body.

- Squeeze quickly, to a degree just enough to compress your cat's chest to about half its normal capacity.

- Try to get into a rhythm between breathing and compression. You want to compress your cat's chest 15 times every ten seconds. In the meantime, try to breathe into your cat's nose after every 10 compressions.

Checking for Signs

After a minute, recheck your cat for signs of breathing and heart beat. It is possible that it has started breathing while you were administering CPR. If not, repeat the process 10 times, over 10 minutes. If there is no sign of breathing after this, unfortunately it is unlikely to return.

If you are successful in resuscitating your cat, remember to take it to the veterinary surgery as soon as possible. For help in doing this, see the next chapter of our guide, *Transporting Your Cat Safely*.

At the Vet's

Once you've reached the veterinary surgery, the vet on duty will examine your cat before they take any further steps. They will assess the condition of your cat's heart and lungs, to see if they should proceed with their own resuscitation efforts. Be prepared for this, as the vet may decide you have done all that could be done.

If they do proceed with further resuscitation, and revive your cat, they will then carry out further tests to see if there are any underlying health problems. If you have taken resuscitation steps because your cat was choking, you might find this confusing. In fact, this is the perfect time to find out if your cat is otherwise healthy.

Your vet's CPR treatment will be different to that of your own first aid efforts. As they are the experts, and have all the latest equipment, this is only to be expected. The following are standard procedures in veterinary surgeries:

- **Endotracheal Tube.** This is a much more efficient means of getting air into your cat's body than blowing through its nose. The tube delivers oxygen directly to the lungs, via your cat's trachea.

- **Intravenous Catheter.** This very minor procedure allows easier administration of emergency medication, and can be used to rehydrate your cat.

- **Epinephrine** is a powerful drug, delivered through the intravenous catheter, which stimulates both your cat's heart and its breathing.

6

Transporting
Your Cat Safely

Applying first aid to your cat is an excellent first step in ensuring its full recovery from illness or injury. In many cases, however, it is just that; a first step. Most of the time, as you will read in this guide, the first aid treatment is completed by a trip to the veterinary surgery. Just as you wouldn't trust yourself to cure your family of many of the ailments described here, so you should entrust the health of your cat to the professionals.

In fact, transporting your cat safely is an excellent first aid skill to have generally. You may need to take your cat to many places, not just to the vet. Cats are designed to prowl and roam free, not sit in cages looking out of windows. For this reason, they can become distressed when forced into such a situation. While you know it's for their own good, they don't.

Learning how to get your cat safely from a to b while not under its own devices could serve both you and it well in the future.

The Right Carrier

Being transported in a vehicle is one of the least likely things a cat was ever designed for. Being curious, self-reliant creatures, they will naturally wonder what is going on every second of the way. This may be helped by them not feeling well, but on the other hand, that could make the situation worse. If your cat is distressed, any extra stress will add to its anxiety. Having a cat carrier which your pet is used to will make taking it to the vet or anywhere else much, much easier.

As there is an ever growing range of cat carriers to choose from, here are essentials to help you choose the right one for you and your pet:

1 **Quality.** As cats are strong, willful animals with sharp teeth and claws, your cat carrier will have to be well made. This means having a mesh your cat can't break through, as well as nothing it can harm itself on in the interior. You will also need a carrier with excellent seams, be they stitched, zipped or held with Velcro. Remember, you are carrying both a carrier and your cat at the same time. If your pet is on the large side, you won't have the luxury of cradling it in your arms as usual.

2 **Size.** Your carrier is not a cage, even though it will have grilles. Your cat needs to have enough room to move freely, even if it can't. Remember, cats need their space, wherever they are.

Being transported in a vehicle is one of the least likely things a cat was ever designed for. Being curious, self-reliant creatures, they will naturally wonder what is going on every second of the way.

3 Handles and Shoulder Straps. Taking control of a cat in its carrier is not always easy. Even a shopping bag with similar weight wouldn't be the easiest thing to carry. Bearing in mind you have a sick, living animal in what is essentially a box with you, it's best to have all the tools necessary. Maneuvering from your home to your vehicle, then out again into the veterinary surgery, takes some consideration. Think about how far your vehicle is from your home, and also where you are likely to be able to park at the other end. Carrying equipment such as handles and straps should be of the highest quality.

Getting Acquainted

So that your cat is as comfortable as possible when being transported, it should be well used to its carrier. Getting inside it should be as much as possible part of your pet's normal routine. This avoids adding stress to a first aid or emergency situation.

Ideally, your cat should see the carrier as part of its home. Keep it in the same place, as part of the furniture. Have it open at all times, so your cat can explore it like it would anywhere else. It may well choose to spend time there at certain times of the day.

You could also put a blanket in there, and maybe some toys. You may find that it puts its own favorites in there of its own accord. This is a sign that your cat is comfortable being in its carrier. Remember, cats have a superb sense of smell, and will detect foreign objects immediately. Anything connected with your pet's carrier should be familiar to it, so its senses don't react adversely when the time comes to use the carrier.

In Transit

When actually taking your cat anywhere in its carrier, try to make the experience as stress free as possible. Make sure your pet is comfortable inside the carrier, whether it needs protection with a towel, or can move more freely. When you get your cat and carrier into your vehicle, make sure you leave it there. Don't be tempted to let your cat out of its carrier to have a bit more room. Even on non-essential journeys, this is a bad idea. Just because there is more room inside your vehicle, doesn't mean you should let your cat explore it.

When you have the carrier in place, secure it properly. Whether this is in the back seat, or you have a hatchback or bigger area, use the appropriate belts and anchor points. Some modern vehicles come with specially designed harnesses and / or belts which will accommodate a cat carrier.

- **Do not** place your carrier in a closed trunk of any kind. If you have a vehicle with carrying facilities for other purposes, don't be tempted to put your cat and carrier in there. Cats will panic in a dark, moving box, however short the journey. This could seriously compromise their health, especially when they are already ill and distressed.

- **Remember air bags.** If you have to put your cat carrier in the front passenger seat, remember to disable the air bag on that side. As air bags can activate very quickly in all sorts of circumstances, don't take the risk of your passenger air bag doing this while your poorly cat is in its carrier. Your cat could be injured by being thrown around inside its carrier, and certainly won't feel any better for the experience.

Once you've reached the veterinary surgery, the vet on duty will examine your cat before they take any further steps. They will assess the condition of your cat's heart and lungs, to see if they should proceed with their own resuscitation efforts. Be prepared for this, as the vet may decide you have done all that could be done.

If they do proceed with further resuscitation, and revive your cat, they will then carry out further tests to see if there are any underlying health problems. If you have taken resuscitation steps because your cat was choking, you might find this confusing. In fact, this is the perfect time to find out if your cat is otherwise healthy.

Your vet's CPR treatment will be different to that of your own first aid efforts. As they are the experts, and have all the latest equipment, this is only to be expected. The following are standard procedures in veterinary surgeries:

- **Endotracheal Tube.** This is a much more efficient means of getting air into your cat's body than blowing through its nose. The tube delivers oxygen directly to the lungs, via your cat's trachea.

- **Intravenous Catheter.** This very minor procedure allows easier administration of emergency medication, and can be used to rehydrate your cat.

- **Epinephrine** is a powerful drug, delivered through the intravenous catheter, which stimulates both your cat's heart and its breathing.

Warning: Unfortunately, the nature of a cat's cardiovascular system means that, if CPR becomes necessary, your cat is unlikely to survive. If it does, it will be very ill for some time. Your vet will keep your cat in hospital conditions, until they are satisfied that all tests have been completed. The financial implications of all of this will be broached by your vet, which is something you need to be prepared for.

7

Pet Insurance
for your Cat

Pet insurance is very popular these days as it can cover those high-priced illnesses or incidents that come along that can be difficult for the average person to afford unexpectedly. There are many pets given up to rescue centers because their owners simply cannot afford them. Imagine your cat needs a surgery and it is thousands of pounds. If you have pet insurance that covers the surgery, it can be a relief. Otherwise, you have some hard decisions to make if you cannot afford it.

Pros of obtaining pet insurance

- There are a lot of great reasons to purchase pet insurance. We have some listed here:

- Pet insurance can give you some peace of mind. If your cat unexpectedly needs a major surgery or gets a serious injury, the cost will be covered by pet insurance.

- Any ongoing conditions your cat gets after you start the insurance will be covered up to the highest amount offered in your policy.

- There are some pet insurance policies that cover if your cat is the cause of a car accident and will pay to repair the driver's car and handle personal injuries the driver may have. These policies can be more expensive but are something to look into.

- If you keep up your payments for your pet insurance, your cat will be covered for life which will cover any vet bills allowed in the policy.

- Some pet insurance providers will cover alternative remedies such as acupuncture and herbal medicine.

- If you insure more than one pet, you might be entitled to a discount for pet insurance.

Cons of obtaining pet insurance

- You can possibly be charged more for older cats.

- Certain breeds that need special care might be charged more for.

- Some pet insurance charges more for un-neutered or un-spayed cats as they can have more health issues as discussed in our spay and neuter section.

- Many pet insurers do not cover pre-existing conditions for around 12 months before you purchased the policy. So, if your cat had any symptoms of a disease or condition or your vet advised they had a condition during that time they might not cover it. Speak with the insurer to go over this portion to make sure you understand what is covered or not.

- It is usual for a lot of pet insurance companies to not pay for any injuries or illnesses that occur during the first 14 days of coverage.

There are so many providers on the market at this time. It is worth your time to contact at least a few insurers and compare prices and coverage.

Different kinds of policies

There are usually three different types of pet insurance:

- **Coverage for the life of your pet.** This coverage covers the most illnesses and will cover them for the life of your pet.

- **Policy per condition.** This is a limited policy and will only cover a condition until the limit has been met. You cannot later claim for the condition again.

- **A yearly policy.** These policies only cover one year at a time, and there is a set amount you can claim per condition. Any treatment beyond that fixed amount, you will need to pay for. Also, per condition, you can claim only one time. If your cat ends up with a long-term illness, this policy is not for you. All in all, the safest policy is the one with lifelong coverage.

What is the best deal?

There are so many providers on the market at this time. It is worth your time to contact at least a few insurers and compare prices and coverage. Also, ask friends and your vet for recommendations. A few popular plans are Direct Line Pet Insurance, Petplan, Animal Friends, John Lewis Finance Pet Insurance, and PDSA. **www.confused.com** is a good place to compare quotes if you do not want to contact each provider individually. You can also compare at **www.petinsuranceonline.co.uk** to check different categories of coverage.

What to ask pet insurance companies

Potential pet insurance companies can send you a document showing you what will be covered. If you do not understand the policy or have questions you need to always feel free to ask. Some possible questions that may help are:

Q. What is covered in my policy?

A. Never assume a thing when it comes to pet insurance. There are cheaper plans that can end up being of very little value to the pet owner in the long run. Ask if your insurer covers more than vet bills. Some will cover fees to board your cat at a cattery or compensate you if your cat gets ill and your holiday has to be canceled.

Also, some policies cover 'third party liability.' This is helpful if your pet is the cause of any accident your cat causes that results in property damage or death. Usually, your pet insurance will pay your legal fees and will compensate the party that is suing you. There is often an excess applied to a lot of the claims you make.

Q. Is this policy a 'covered for life' policy?

A. With the 'covered for life' policy any long-term illness will be covered over and over. However, there is a limit to how much they pay out each year. This is the most complete kind of pet insurance but also the most costly. If this is what you are looking for, make sure to confirm it with the insurer. It might be a good idea to consider the 'covered for life' policy if you can afford it, especially before anything comes up due to pre-existing conditions not always being covered in some policies.

Q. What is not covered in my policy?

A. Ask what is not covered. Some policies will only pay for a condition once per year. Others will only reimburse for the first year of your cat's sickness. For long-term illnesses, this would not be ideal.

Q. No matter what treatment really costs, will this policy only pay for a certain percentage for some illnesses?

A. It is important to ask this. The surgery may cost £2000. However, your insurer may only pay out £1200. Do not assume that every pound is paid out.

Q. What is the process for making a claim for vet's fees?

A. With most pet insurance you pay the vet, and the insurer reimburses you via a claim form. There are some insurance companies that will let your vet directly bill them. Your policy should list this procedure.

8

More About Cats

Stolen or lost cats

If your cat does go missing, it can have you frantic. Hopefully, you will have microchipped your cat and put a collar with a name/number tag on your pooch. If your cat goes missing:

- Look for your cat in all of the places they love to go, such as within its territory.

- Call all vets in the area you live in. Sometimes people take cats they find into vets.

- Call or go down to the cat Warden Service for your area.

- Go door to door with a picture of your cat asking if anyone has seen it. Bring slips of paper with your phone number to give them if they do.

- Make some 'Lost cat' posters, preferably with a photo of your cat. Now that you are reading this, if you have not already, take some good photos of your cat. Also, add the word 'REWARD' to your posters and do not specify the amount. If you are on a budget, a reward can be £20. It seems people pay more attention to the word REWARD in all caps. I once found an elderly woman's cat after seeing a poster. I did not accept the reward and was just happy for her to be with her cat. So, some people may not even take the money.

- Call the police! Sometimes people bring lost cats to the police station as there are scanners for microchips there.

- Place an advertisement in your local paper or ask local shops if you can pop a lost cat poster in their window or on their noticeboard.

- There are websites such as **Tabby Tracker** where you can register that you have lost your cat. **www.nationalpetsregister.org** is another pet registry you can use (the UK National Pets Register.) Animal shelters, vets, police and ordinary folks across the UK check there daily. These are free services.

- Make sure to have an updated name tag on your cat's collar with name and phone number. You can also include an address. These times are when it is good to have spent the small amount to microchip your cat for peace of mind.

Adopting a cat

There are often cats at rescue centers or special cats breed rescues that would love a home with you. It is always worth thinking about adopting a cat rather than buying one. Visit your local rescue center to see if they have any cats available. Many times, people cannot keep up with a cat's needs. If you are game for it, then you might be this cat's dream home. You will find cats at breed-specific rescues.

Adopting a cat will usually involve an adoption fee to cover costs and help the other homeless animals. You will be asked a lot of questions, but that is good for the animal being adopted as they can make sure you and the cat you want will be a good fit. Most rescues will do a check of your home to make sure it is a good place for the cat you are adopting. Many times, just agreeing to the home check shows you are serious. During home checks, rescues can also give suggestions for things you can do to make sure your cat will be healthy, happy and safe.

Many people tend to have a cat-sitter come to their home to care for their cat, or they take their cat to catteries when they are going away on a trip.

Traveling with your cat

Many people tend to have a cat-sitter come to their home to care for their cat, or they take their cat to catteries when they are going away on a trip. However, sometimes people want to take their cat with them. Others are moving permanently and, of course, want to take their cat to their new home. Here are a few tips below.

Catteries and cat-sitters

- Ask people you trust for recommendations for a good pet-sitter or catteries.

- A Pet-sitter will be coming into your home. You need someone trustworthy. Make sure the pet sitter is insured for liability, including care, custody, and control of your cat. Make sure to get a signed copy of your pet-sitting contract with the pet-sitter. Make sure the pet-sitter knows pet first aid and has a backup plan in case they have a personal emergency.

- For catteries, you need to check that they are licensed and insured for liability, including care, custody, and control of your cat. Also, visit the facility to see where your cat will be staying. Ask the catteries how much attention your cat will receive. Ask if there is a discount on price if you provide your cat's food. It is good to keep your cat on the same food to not have too many changes at once while you are gone.

- If you decide on using a cattery, then bring your cat's favorite blanket, food, and toys, so they have familiar items with them in their new environment. This will help ease stress for your cat.

Flying with your cat

If you do decide to fly with your cat, you need to plan ahead of time. To make things simple, you can use an agency that helps fly pets. They will do a lot of the work for you and guide you through everything for a fee. If the fee is affordable, this can be good for someone pressed with time. In 2004 The Pet Travel Scheme was introduced to stop pets from having to go through the stress of quarantine if certain requirements were met. This scheme only has certain countries participating such as the UK and the EU. There are certain time schedules for vaccinations, and pet passports so plan well ahead. For more information on the travel scheme, please go to this website **https://www.gov.uk/take-pet-abroad** and this website **http://apha.defra.gov.uk/external-operations-admin/library/documents/exports/ET159.pdf**